the little book of miracles

by
M.M. van Rensburg

ISBN: 978-1-7397184-6-6

Meditate

sometimes we need a little miracle

that

יהוה

HOLY HOLY HOLY
is Hashem Tzva'ot
(Isaiah 6:3a).

אדני

as you scan the chart from right to left

remember

we have an ever

present help in our time of need

והו	ילי	סיט	עלם	מהש	ללה	אכא	כהת
הזי	אלד	לאו	ההע	יזל	מבה	הרי	הקם
לאו	כלי	לוו	פהל	נלך	ייי	מלה	חהו
נתה	האא	ירת	שאה	ריי	אום	לכב	ושר
יחו	להח	כוק	מנד	אני	חעם	רהע	ייז
ההה	מיכ	וול	ילה	סאל	ערי	עשל	מיה
והו	דני	החש	עמם	ננא	נית	מבה	פוי
נמם	ייל	הרח	מצר	ומב	יהה	ענו	מחי
דמב	מנק	איע	חבו	ראה	יבמ	היי	מום

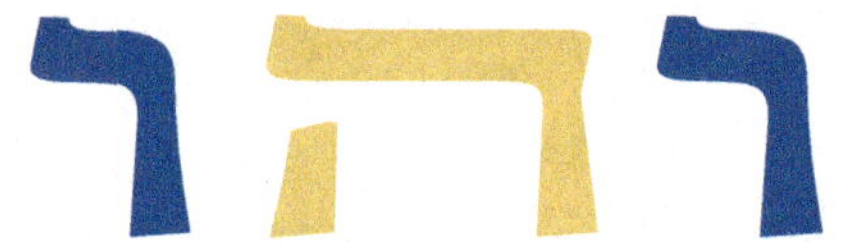

help i feel as if my life is timeworn, meaningless, temporal and broken

as i meditate on this holy
name וֹהוֹ
i am forever connected
to the *Grace Breath*
of incessant Love

help i feel depleted as
if my life force is frag–
mented and something is
missing

as i meditate on this holy name ילי

i am restored in the hands of the

Good Shepherd

T

help i feel dull and stuck
and sorry for myself as if
i have lost my potency

as i meditate on this holy

name סיט

i am awakened to the

Glory spark of the river

of life stirring inside

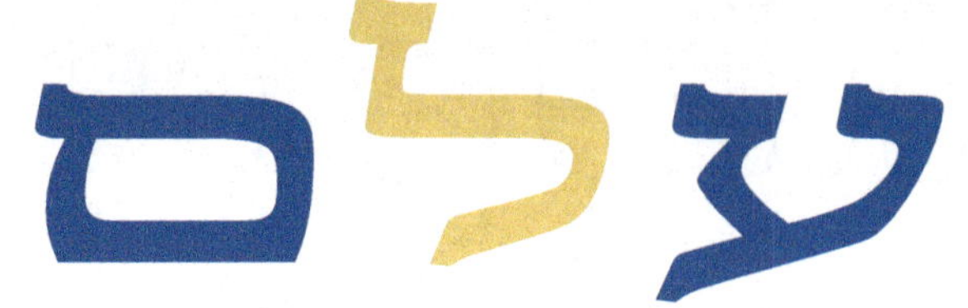

help i have so many negative thoughts rush–ing through my mind as i meditate on this holy name שלם

my mind is calmed by the

Illuminating Mirror

of Peace

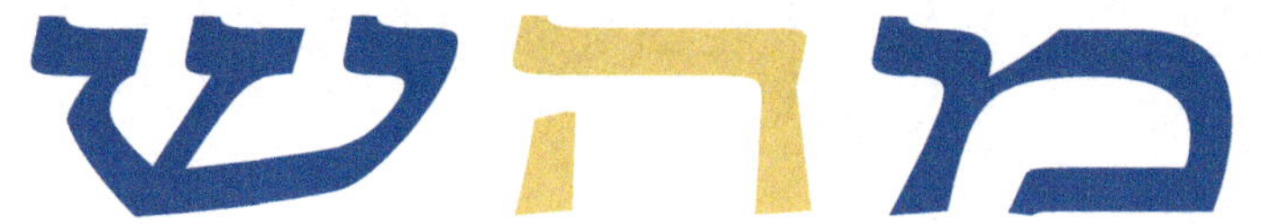

help i feel sick and tired;
my body is in pain and
my life is out of balance

as i meditate on this holy

name מהש

i feel the healing peace

of the *Glory Wind*

help i can't sleep; i lie awake at night and in the daytime i am tired and unmotivated

as i meditate on this holy

name לאה

i begin to dream again

as the

Faithful Shepherd

comforts me

help nothing makes sense; there is no order in my life– i am drifting

as i meditate on this holy name אבא
i am realigned; held to-
gether in the open
hand of the *Perfect One*

יד

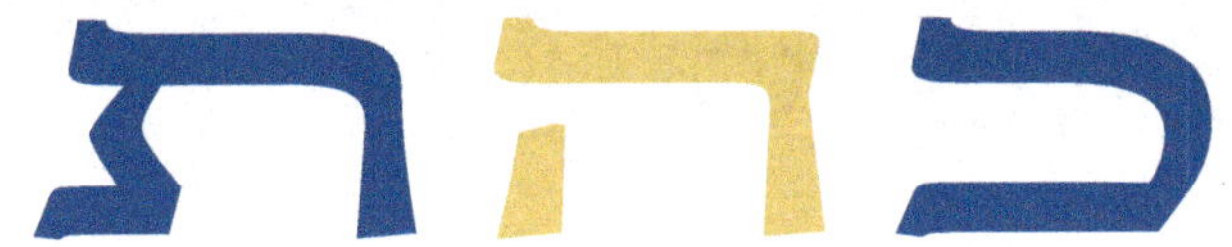

help i feel stressed and this is magnified by my environment

יה

as i meditate on this holy name כהת

i drink from the tranquil

Breath of Peace

יו

help i am struggling to cope and feel as if my life is in danger as i meditate on this holy name הזי

i am protected by the

sword breaths of Yah

help i see wrong every–
where and am not sure
whether i can trust peo–
ple anymore

as i meditate on this holy name אלד *supernal Wisdom* pro–tects me from all evil in–tentions towards me

כ

help my environment feels dark and is making me nervous

as i meditate on this holy name לאו

the energy around me is cleansed by the *Almighty Breath*

help i feel betrayed and rejected by someone i thought was my friend as i meditate on this holy name עהה

i behold the beauty of and splendour of

undeserving Love

כד

help the world around me looks dismal and i am unable to do any–thing about it as i meditate on this holy name יזל

i realise the power for change is a *holy weapon* within

help there is so much animosity in the world, it is wearing me down as i meditate on this holy name מבה

i take my own chaos into the *House of peace*

and breathe again

כח

help my life is lacking di–
rection and i am unable
to envision anything for
my future

as i meditate on this holy
name יהוה
i see beyond what is and
back to the
of who I am *first spark*

help i feel sad and down all the time and i can't seem to shake it off as i meditate on this holy name הקם

i see the *horizon*

as i lift my gaze towards King Messiah

help sometimes i am so selfish and self centred, it is hard to let go as i meditate on this holy name לאו

i am taken up into the

One who gave his all for me

לד

help i dont see any fruit
in anything i do,
everything is dying
around me

as i meditate on this holy name כלי

i am lead into

blissful creative

Shechinah Glory

help it feels as if God has abandoned me and i have no access to him

as i meditate on this holy
name לזר
i enter into the aware-
ness of my *unity*
with the King of Glory

help i have habbits that are preventing me from moving forward in my life

לט

as i meditate on this holy name

פהל

i see

Creative solutions

and blessings

unfolding before me

help i am surrounded by so much infectious dis-ease and stagnation as i meditate on this holy name נלך

i awaken my conscious-ness to the path of *Abounding Life* in me

help i keep attracting the wrong people and cir– cumstances into my life as i meditate on this holy name ייי

i am filled with the

holy sparks of The

Endless Light

help i say silly things that i regret afterwards and it makes me feel dull and lifeless

מה

as i meditate on this holy
name מלה
i begin to speak in the
heart desire of the
voice of Love

help i keep compar–
ing myself to others and
feeling jealous of what
they have

מז

as i meditate on this holy name יהוה i am embraced by the *The Comforter* as i behold a new day

מח

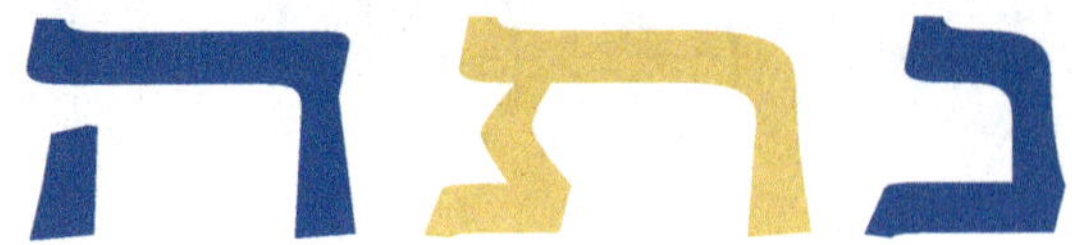

help i am unable to say
what i think like a mute
mouth in exile

as i meditate on this holy name נתה

i am encouraged by the *promise* of the Living Word in my every breath

help i feel like everything around me is in a state of chaos

as i meditate on this holy
name הֵאָא
i receive a *blueprint*
from the Perfect Prince
of Peace

help i am stressed and broke and never seem to have enough

as i meditate on this holy
name ירת
i begin to *partner* with
the Giver of abundant
promises

help i feel incapabe of forming deep connec–tions with other people

as i meditate on this holy

name שאה

i feel *desire dancing* in

the flaming breath of the

silent kiss of Love

help i don't like certain people and can't tolerate being near them as i meditate on this holy name ריי

i am reconnected to

to Love as *the Light*

illumes my heart

נח

help i am offended and have been mistreated by certain people as i meditate on this holy name אום

i am *one* with all, as i resonate with the har–mony of Heaven

help i keep procrastinat-
ing and i am losing my
desire to keep going

as i meditate on this holy name

לכב

i know the *Faithful One*

will complete the good work begun in me

help i have flashbacks and i can't seem to let go of the images in my mind

as i meditate on this holy

name רשו

i feel a *holy fire* re–

vealing the true essence

of my life song

TO

help i feel trapped in a cycle of wrong decisions and negative situations as i meditate on this holy name יחו

i am liberated by the light of the *Righteous One*

help i continuously clash with people and feel i need to do things my way or the highway

as i meditate on this holy name לזהח

i breathe out self as i am breathed by the

Selfless Breath

no

help i am disinterested in life and relationships and lack creative flow

as i meditate on this holy

name כוק

i am entwined with the

Infinite Intelligence

of everything

ע

help i am nervous and afraid and seem to have lost my courage

as i meditate on this holy
name מנד
i let go of fear and dive
through the open portal
of *Eternal Life*

עב

help i feel stuck in a rut;
i am in a maze and i
don't know which way to
turn

עג

as i meditate on this holy
name אני
i *elevate* above the ca–
cophony of noise and
see with fresh eyes

עד

help i am hesitant to give of myself and even more hesitant to receive

עה

as i meditate on this holy

name חעם

i experience the power

of being continuously

connected to the limitless

help i feel like i am slow–
ly dying inside; my life
is empty and nothing is
how i imagined it to be

עז

as i meditate on this holy

name עהר

i begin to shine as i

manifest beauty from

the ashes in my life

עח

help i keep blurting out
inappropriate statements
and can't seem to say
the right thing

עט

as i meditate on this holy name

זלך

i am *empowered* to

speak from the heart as

i create with my words

help i feel like a victim
and i often put myself
down; i lack lustre

as i meditate on this holy name ההה

i am dazzled by the *Grace-life* that pos–sesses me within

help i feel like i need to escape from the reali–ty of my life; i haven't a clue what's going on

as i meditate on this holy

name מיכ

i gain *deeper insight*

i see myself and am not

afraid

ררל

help i feel like i want
to break free but don't
know how; i am so dull
and earth bound

as i meditate on this holy name וול

i am *liberated* from the illusionary chains that hold me back

help i feel guilty and not good enough – i fail the "good person" test; i feel like a lost cause as i meditate on this holy name יזלה

i am *exonerated* and am able to forgive myself and others

help i never seem to
have enough to get by
and am struggling to pay
my way in life

as i meditate on this holy name סאל

i am connected to

Prosperity and wealth

that lies within

צ

help i am wavering in my faith and sometimes wonder if God is really in control as i meditate on this holy name עזרי

i am reminded that *Adonai is*

the I AM of my life

צב

עשל

help i am perturbed by
the state of the world;
things seem to be going
from bad to worse

צג

as i meditate on this holy

name עשל

i am *reignited* with

the consciousness that

peace begins within

צד

help i am feeling isolat–
ed and separate from
the world and the people
around me

צה

as i meditate on this holy

name מיה

i am aware of *oneness*

as i celebrate and share

breath with everyone

help i feel dissatisfied
with who i am and un–
happy with what life has
thrown at me

as i meditate on this holy
name יהוה
i am *overwhelmed* by
the great price that was
paid for my miracle joy

צח

help i am underachiev–
ing and aimless; i am
living my second best
life and don't really care

צט

as i meditate on this holy

name דבי

i am *joyfully jolted*

as i see my life scroll

open before me

help i am experiencing remorse and feel guilty for all the wrong i have done

as i meditate on this holy
name שחה
i am *washed* in the liv–
ing breath of the holy
flame of Yah

help i am distracted and
my desire for my first
Love is growing cold

as i meditate on this holy

name עמס

i am intoxicated by the

wonder of the

Mysterious One

קד

help i am becoming egocentric and brazen–ly opportunistic towards others as i meditate on this holy name נבא

i am humbly moved to *love lavishly* and un–conditionally

help i am surrounded by
the illusion of death and
a death consciousness
wherever i go

as i meditate on this holy name נית

i am *energised* by the grace covenant of im–
mortality

help i am full of ideas yet unable to actualise anything

קט

as i meditate on this holy

name מבה

i am *united* in thought

and speech resulting in

powerful action

help i am so furious i
want to scream and do
not want to say some-
thing i will regret later

רא

as i meditate on this holy
name פרי
i *speak* blessing in–
stead of cursing and my
ego is subdued

help i feel as if i am drifting – there are so many conflicting voices in my head; i cant hear as i meditate on this holy name נמם

i *join* my waters to the waters of the Throne of Glory and all is clear

רד

help i am feeling a strong desire to hold onto what i know, and to stay in the safe zone

רה

as i meditate on this holy
name ייל
i *jump* into an open
space, pulling my future
into the now

ח

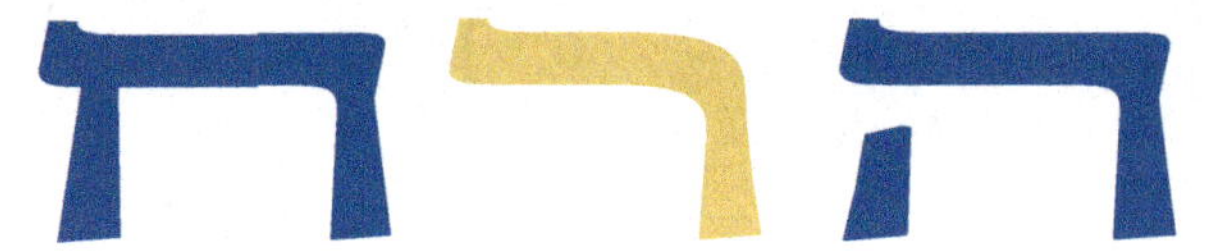

help i am feeling discon–
nected and alone in the
dark and far away from
God

as i meditate on this holy
name הרה
i am *nurtured* in the
holy sanctum of divine
Light

רח

help i am trapped in my
own world of selfish dis–
ilusionment and limita–
tions

as i meditate on this holy name

מצר

i am able to

soar

eage–like into true Free–dom

ש

ומב

help humanity is pollut–
ing the ocean and dis–
respecting the waters;
mercy has receded

שא

as i meditate on this holy

name ומב

i become a *conduit*

of healing between the

upper and lower waters

שב

help i am not getting
through to anybody; i
come across as a loud–
mouthed know it all

שג

as i meditate on this holy
name יהה
i become a *fountain*
of inspiration and
miracle revelation to all

שד

עבר

help i am like an un-
grateful child; i am never
satisfied with what i have

שה

as i meditate on this holy
name עבר
i am *humbly* moved by
the revelation of sacred
Love come down

שו

מחי

help i am giving out negative vibes and no one wants to be around me

שז

as i meditate on this holy
name מחי
i am *renewed* and feel
secure in myself to share
the best of me

שח

help i am becoming too familiar with the holiness of the Creator as i meditate on this holy name דמב

i enter into true Wisdom through the *Awe* of the Father of Glory

help i am feeling chaotic inside, and i am not sure if i can thrive in this life; there is no exit

תא

as i meditate on this holy name מנק
i am able to plant *seeds*
of change that will lead
to a new reality

תב

help i am unable to live up to the expectations i put upon myself and others

תג

as i meditate on this holy

name עיא

i am *inspired* to step

into the higher calling

that i was created for

תד

help i am unable to let go of my loved one, i feel them still and am afraid i will forget them

תה

as i meditate on this holy name חבו

i am *comforted* that life never ends; in the house of Glory we will all meet

תו

help i am so lost; there
are so many things vi–
aing for my attention
and it all feels hazy

תז

as i meditate on this holy name ראה

i am *reunited* with vision and purpose and new inner strength

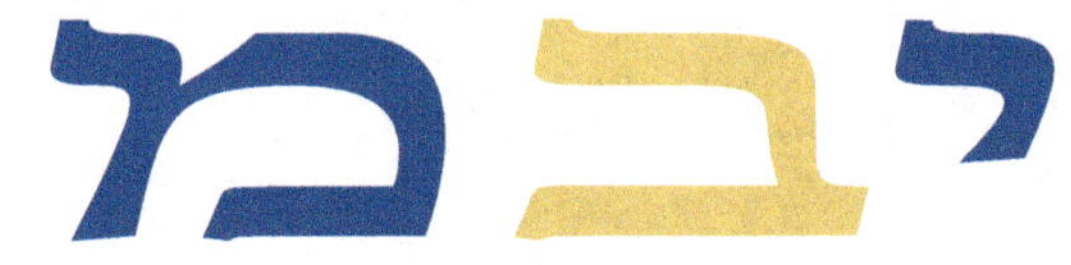

help i am all over the place; days are passing and i need to get a grip of things as i meditate on this holy name יבמ

i am *translocated* by Prudence into the realm of clarity

help i am frustrated with the illusion of what is; i just know that there is more to all this as i meditate on this holy name ייה

i enter through the portal of the side of Love into the *Endless*

תקב

help i am con–
science–stricken and re–
morsful; and the earth
screams out: soiled

as i meditate on this holy name מזם

i become a conduit of *Grace* in the purity and beauty of Yah

תקד

יהוה

The whole earth is full of his GLORY (Isaiah 6:3b).

אדני

Shechinah Glory manfest in us today

Shalom

other books written by the author:

Awakening the memory of the soul: 216 mystical poems inspired by the 72 Names of YHVH

The 72 Awesome Names of God series for kids:

BooK 1 VAV HEY VAV

Book 2 YOD LAMED YOD

תקח

Printed in Great Britain
by Amazon